The Girl at the Lion d'Or
A Fool's Alphabet
Birdsong
The Fatal Englishman
Charlotte Gray
On Green Dolphin Street
Human Traces
Engleby
A Week in December

SEBASTIAN FAULKS

PISTACHE

arrow books

Published by Arrow Books 2010

2 4 6 8 10 9 7 5 3 1

Copyright © Sebastian Faulks 2006
Illustrations © George Papadakis 2006

First published in Great Britain in 2006 by
Hutchinson
Random House, 20 Vauxhall Bridge Road,
London SW1V2SA

www.rbooks.co.uk

Addresses for companies within The Random House Group Limited can be found at:
www.randomhouse.co.uk/offices.htm

The Random House Group Limited Reg. No. 954009

A CIP catalogue record for this book
is available from the British Library

ISBN 9780099549499

The Random House Group Limited supports The Forest Stewardship Council (FSC),
the leading international forest certification organisation. All our titles that are
printed on Greenpeace approved FSC certified paper carry the FSC logo.
Our paper procurement policy can be found at www.rbooks.co.uk/environment

To A.T.F.
The Master

With thanks to *Write Stuff* producers Katie Marsden, Dawn Ellis and Jon Rolph; readers Beth Chalmers and Becky Hindley; to the guests over nine series; and especially to buzzer-gods James Walton and John Walsh.

KINGSLEY AMIS

has a shot at a female narrator

Joshua, typically, still hadn't telephoned when I got back from work. Since the old Nag's Head, a passable Victorian boozer with a regular and satisfied clientele, was naturally deemed ripe for transformation into a 'Men's Outreach Centre', I had instead to go to the local wine bar, Tossers or Prats or some such name. Here I passed a moderately entertaining evening with Philippa, who managed to avoid buying me a drink for almost two hours as we wondered what it would be like to be a PE teacher in a boys' school.

A young man presumably interested in the only thing young men have any interest in, attempted to start a conversation with us.

'Where were you bought up?' he asked, implying that I had been bartered as a child in some Alexandrian slave market.

'I was b*rrrr*ought up in South London,' I corrected him.

He looked puzzled. 'That's like, cool?' he said. 'Near the Tate Modern? That's like, iconic?'

'Are you asking me or telling me?' I said.

'I'm like, asking you?'

However, the little shit did buy me half a dozen Glen Larghaigs, after which it seemed only reasonable to invite him back to share the magnum of quite passable Chilean pinot I had bought from Brobdingnag's Volume Discount.

I awoke next morning with the feeling that an entire pack of foxhounds had used my mouth as, consecutively, kennel, latrine and exercise yard and were now taking it in turns to cross-examine me.

The source of the questions turned out to be little Darren or Darryl from Tossers, who was unaccountably in my bed, shaking my shoulder and asking if I would care for some 'like, tea?'.

I dressed as fast as I could in a paisley shirtwaister from the outsize shop on Haverstock Hill called, unbelievably, All Bra None. My arse looked enormous, like the rear end of, say, a handsomely, though not exceptionally, endowed Ugandan flabhog.

At this moment, typically, Joshua chose to pay his weekly, unannounced, visit. After I had given him a brief and highly selective account of the night's events, he told me how 'let down' he felt, then went home in tears.

And bloody good luck to you, chum, I thought.

MARTIN AMIS

sends his lad to Hogwarts

◄○►

Primped and shining in the school's idea of a uniform – to which my success in the risibly straightforward scholarship exam had condemned me – I was presented to 'Professor' McGonagall, a chestless sexagenarian with halitosis that could have downed a wing of Lancasters; then to Dumbledore, the shuffling dotard of a headmaster, whose eyes appraised me with the unhurried insolence of the career pederast.

He entrusted me to Hermione Granger, a smug little number with a row of coloured gel pens in the pocket of her Aertex shirt, an item given pleasing heft by the twin discs of her tumid little breasts. She was, I had already been told, rumoured to give hand jobs of Stakhanovite efficiency to the gods of the Quidditch team as they showered off the stardust of their sporting triumphs, lined up in engorged single file.

The dormitory was a row of iron beds, purchased at some Gulag boot sale; the wanking opportunities, doubtless in breach of numerous human rights, looked about as promising as those in a lock-down facility for convicted Islamic pickpockets.

Next from that baleful twilight emerged 'Ron' Weasley, a spavined welterweight who reeked of chav, with his fucked-up bathmat of orange frizz and his eyes full of cancelled hope. In the bed next to mine was Harry Potter, a

3

weapons-grade geek with a thunderbolt of acne through his candidly sebaceous forehead, who told me he lived in a *cupboard* for fuck's sake.

Outside, I waved goodbye to my parents with sinister, *noir*-ish gestures, the sculpted rhomboids of my fingernails still glistening from the manicure they had received that morning from Renska, the tragically unmagnetic Pole in Hans 'n' Feat on Ken High Street, who had more or less begged me to let her go down on my, admittedly, triangulated groin.

'Gosh,' said little Potter. 'I hope you'll be in Gryffindor.'

'I think not,' I said, watching as the witch McGonagall embarked on some embarrassing hokum with an oldster's rug-covering into which she periodically plunged her veiny claw.

I had been given the low-down on the houses by one Malfoy, an enthusiastic sodomite in the second year, whose parents knew mine through some unspeakable, almost certainly adulterous, connection of tennis and 'pot-luck' suppers, for which Mrs M favoured pleated white skirts of possibly illegal brevity, granting occasional glimpses of white cotton gash that had furnished material for an entire summer of jackhammer fantasy.

And so it was that at the end of my first day, answering wearily to the call of my name, I pulled myself up to my full four feet eleven and sauntered through the porter's lodge to Slytherin, its turbid quadrangles, its simmering ante-rooms . . .

JANE AUSTEN
steps out with an American Psycho

Mr Bateman was said to have a fortune in excess of five million pounds a year from his employment in the counting house of a usurers in the lower part of Manhattan Island; which sum enabled him to venture forth that Wednesday night in a suit of clothes made for him by Thomas Clark Esq. of Madison Avenue, a tie of a design by Mr Sandor Ferenczi, a pair of buttoned boots bespoke from Lowell & Andrews of Beacon Hill, Boston and undergarments fashioned by his grandfather's slaves on the plantations of Lauren, Alabama.

At dinner in the Chinese establishment of Mr Wu upon Park Avenue, Mr Bateman became agitated when it was revealed to him that a fellow diner, Mr Kellynch, was in possession of an annual fortune nearly twice as large as his own and moreover affected a tie-clip made by a Miss Sophia Klein, and a belt he had imported from the remote South Sea establishment of Ishiguro Mazuki.

Taking the arm of Miss Woodhouse, his betrothed, Mr Bateman ventured out at once into the night and drove her to her lodging place. It now being past the hour at which the ladies of the Upper East Side were given to dine, and finding himself on the verge of contracting involuntarily a union in which neither his affections nor his financial interests could be said to be served, Mr Bateman had recourse to the servants' quarters from which he returned equipped with implements of the artisan variety, with which, notwithstanding her several admonishments, he set about the young lady until such time as he had both eliminated any chance of an unwise alliance and rendered unnecessary the cold supper that awaited his return to Little Hampton.

'Father,' said Emma, 'I am invited by the Netherfield Ladies to attend a function for the 18–30 summer holiday.'

'My dear Emma,' replied her father. 'Why this gazing to the future? The year is 1814. By 1830 we may all be subjects of the Emperor Bonaparte.'

'But Father, we dance all night by the sea.'

'I never had much opinion of the sea air,' said Mr Woodhouse. 'It is never safe to sit out of doors. And who shall chaperone you?'

'All the Bennet girls will be there, Father, and Miss Bertram and Anne Elliot – and she's twenty-seven! And we drink gallons of water and take little pills.'

'I am pleased to hear there is some medicinal aspect to the entertainment,' said Mr Woodhouse, 'but I counsel you against too much water. It is injurious to the liver.'

When Emma arrived for the festivities upon the Cobb at Lyme she could not help remarking the absence of a band; such music as there was issued from a species of hurdy-gurdy operated by a gentleman from Sir Thomas Bertram's plantations in Antigua.

A young man whose family was not known to the Woodhouses requested the pleasure of a dance, but Emma told him she was engaged by the Reverend Elton for the polka. 'However, sir,' she told him, 'I should be obliged if you were to bear me in mind for the quadrille.'

Emma's mind was thrown into consternation by the noise of the music and it was with relief that she spotted at last a familiar acquaintance emerging from the seaside waters.

'Mr Knightley!' she cried.

'Indeed,' he replied, with an uncommon leer upon his face. 'Though down here they call me "Twice Knightley".'

SAMUEL BECKETT

writes a monologue for Ronnie Corbett

'I came up to my dressing room before the show this evening and I found the producer outside the door sitting in a dustbin.

'Now this was very unusual. He doesn't normally sit in a dustbin till after closing time at the BBC social club.

'No, no, I digress. Lovely chap, the producer. He's got a daughter, called Dolores. She's a big girl for eighteen.

'No. Anyway. "Cheer up," I said. "How's your lovely daughter, how's Dolores? I didn't know you could get that much into a tank top – there's certainly no room left for the gunner."

'So the producer said . . . He said, "I wish you wouldn't talk like that about Dolores. She's gone to Oxford University where she's studying philosophy. She's doing a special paper on nihilism and the existential void. She's been reading *Fear and Trembling* by Kierkegaard."

'"Well," I said, "I can see which bits are trembling but what's she frightened of?"

'No, no. Come on now. Behave. Anyway, the producer says, "Go across the room, pick up the script and have a look. Dolores has had a hand in it."

'So I go across the room, pick up the script and have a look.

9

'Across the top is written in big letters, "Malone Dies."
'I said " *What?* Piggy Malone Dies?"
He said, "Yes! It's the existential void for him and it's goodnight from you." Good night!'

ALAN BENNETT

stirs himself and gets adventurous

◄○►

12 MAY

Mam, out of sympathy for the fact that I was always last to be picked for the choir or the football team at school, has signed me up with the SAS. She thought it stood for Salvation Army Singers. I received the papers this morning and told her I've to go to Baghdad. She said, 'Couldn't you just go to the Alhambra on Armley Road?'

She packed me an emergency kit of Vicks vapour rub and digestives, and put me on the Hercules transport to Basra.

13 MAY

We are in the Sunni triangle. It's a bit like Whingate Junction but with more Americans of course. The barracks are a disgrace. The range wants blackleading and the nets are all grey. I suppose they're too busy killing Iraqis to keep the place up to scratch.

Our commanding officer said Mr Blair is about to invade Iran as well. I blame Mrs Thatcher.

14 May

Sat behind two privates on the top deck of a Humvee.

'I don't hold with fundamentalism myself,' said one.

'No,' said the other, 'since me auntie died I've not been to Mecca once.'

Back in barracks had a letter from Mam saying my book of pay-in slips to the Bradford and Bingley had been voted Waterstone's Book of the Century. Felt rather under-appreciated.

15 May

Stormed Abu Graib Prison. I 'took out' – as I think the expression is – four Shia terrorists and rescued a young Iraqi, no more than a kiddie really, they were holding hostage. The poor lad was naked. I got out Mam's emergency kit and covered the kiddie's privates with a Fig Roll.

Back in barracks had a telegram from Her Majesty asking me to become Knight of the Garter and awarding me Victoria Cross. I am, as ever, the last one to be chosen.

JOHN BETJEMAN

spends Easter on the estate

—◄○►—

High above the rain-washed ring-road, o'er the city's roar
    and crash
The family scales the pungent stairwell for our special Easter
    bash.
Shame the lift is out of order; never mind it keeps us fit.
Kylie's brought a bag of Afghan for a crafty pre-lunch hit.
Let's watch Sky until it's ready; keep a place for Dad to sit.
Warm the sun on pink graffiti; loud the wireless that thumps,
Shares abroad its merry rapping while the tense Alsatian
    dumps
His seasonal gifts into the sandpit, good old Rex's festive
    perk,
In the yard so far below us, where the cheerful motors lurk;
Bright the paintwork on the Nissan, brighter still the stolen
    Merc.

In his love nest down in Peckham, Dad has left his girl
    asleep,
Through the gridlock out to Barking, sees his bronze Toyota
    creep;
A family meal with all united, this is how it's meant to be.
Hasn't seen the wife in ages; never mind, just let them be:
A hero's welcome now awaits him, bearer of the KFC.

In our cosy flatlet gather'd, Sharleen shows her navel stud,
Body pierced like Saint Sebastian, skin still damp with
    teenage blood;
Mum parades her shiny highlights, snowy white from roots
    of coal;
Darren staggers in triumphant – his team won and his the
    goal;
And – joy of Paschal joys exceeding – Gary's joined us on
    parole!

ENID BLYTON

sees the Famous Five grown up

After their success in catching Blackbeard and the Foreign-Looking Man at Smuggler's Cove, the Five found they had been posted to the Anti-Terrorist Squad in London.

'Poo-ee,' said Anne on their first afternoon in the office. 'Let's have a jolly good tidy up, shall we? I'll do the washing up.'

'Shut it,' barked Julian, who had picked up the new office talk. 'You can't wash up a styrofoam cup.'

'Well I've had enough takeaway chips,' said Dick. 'I vote we have a proper picnic with apples and cherry cakes and lemonade.'

Julian was lighting a Benson and Hedges as the phone rang. 'I've got you,' he said grimly into the receiver. '12.05, Westminster Bridge.' He put the receiver down glumly. 'It's a bomb warning,' he elaborated. 'Where's the dog?'

'But, J—Julian,' George stammered, 'Timmy's not trained for this Semtex stuff. I vote—'

'There's no votes any more,' Dick confided. 'But Julian, how do you know it's not a bluff? How do you know it's really them?'

'Because he used the right code,' Julian explained.

'But, Julian,' sobbed Anne, setting to work with a J-cloth

on the Flying Squad divisional ashtray, 'why don't we just arrest their leader?'

Julian banged the table. 'Because', he exploded, 'he's the Minister for Education in Belfast.'

'I say,' expostulated Dick. 'That's a pretty rum show.'

The Brontës
place some lonely hearts ads

Character from *Wuthering Heights*
Orphan gypsy boy, aged 12, from Liverpool seeks loving family for quiet life. Countryside preferred.

Charlotte
Yorkshirewoman, aged 26, bossy, consumptive, plain, seeks bald Belgian pedagogue for weekends of prayer, fasting and possible domination. No Catholics.

Branwell
Halifax railway booking clerk, male, 27, seeks fellow adventurer, interested in: mystic literature, sex, alcohol, opium and railway timetables. No geeks.

Reverend Patrick
Man of the cloth, recently widowed, seeks mother's help-cum-housekeeper to help with lively brood in draughty rectory. GSOH essential!

Anne
Are you my Mr Bounderby? Youngest of three N. Yorks sisters seeks escape from repressive family novel-writing

business. Anything to get away from the daily grind of plots and characterisation! Office or manufacturing work preferred.

CHARACTER FROM *Jane Eyre*
Married woman, 32, recently certified, seeks loft conversion specialist.

DAN BROWN
visits the cash dispenser

———————◄◊►———————

The world-renowned author stabbed his dagger-like debit card into the slot. 'Welcome to NatWest,' barked the blushing grey light of the screen to the forty-two-year-old man. He had only two thoughts.

NatWest is a perfect heptogram.

Scratching his aquiline head, frantically trying to remember a number, the sun came up at last and rained its orange beams on Dan Brown. 'What do you want to do?' asserted the blinking screen. His options were stark for Brown, more than ever now. 'Get Mini Statement'. 'Withdraw Cash'. 'Change PIN'. For what seemed an eternity, trying to remember his PIN, the screen mocked the famous writer.

Someone somewhere knows my four-figure PIN.

Whatever my PIN was once is still my PIN and in some remote safe someone somewhere still knows it.

In Paddington Station, an iconic railway terminal with a glass roof like the bastard offspring of a greenhouse and a railway station, a line of fellow travellers was waiting on Brown. Brown frowned down at his brown shoes and for the hundredth time that morning wondered what destiny may have in store for the Exeter, New Hampshire graduate.

The sandy-haired former plagiarism defendant felt his receding temples pounding in his guts. *Four figures. Four figures, you halfwit*, he almost found himself murmuring in Brown's ear, close at hand.

Tentatively his fingers pounded their remorseless melody upon the NatWest keyboard, numerically. He watched his fingers work with sallow eyes.

He typed in anything, literally anything, desperately. He didn't know what affect it may have.

The headquarters of the Royal Bank of Scotland resides in a hydraulically sealed ninety-eight-storey building guarded by hair-trigger sensitive nuclear firedogs at 4918, 274th Street in Manhattan, America, whose security protocol is known to only six elves whose tongues have been cut out for security by the Cyrenian Knights of Albania, the capital of Greece.

In an instant, the famous writer remembered their bleeding skin from barbed wire.

Of course. They must pass on the secret PIN. An unbroken chain whose links are not forged (not in that sense).

9 . . . 8 . . . 7 . . . 6. His fingers pronounced the Sigma number. The Sigma number was almost impossible to fake, whereby the Liberace Sequence was quite easy to forge for prominent author Dan Brown.

The cash machine cleared its throat and breathed in with a rasping exhalation that seemed to shake its very belly. Then finally it expectorated wheezily up twenty-eight million dollars into the fingers pregnant with expectation of the forty-two-year-old man.

'Take your cash now please,' pleaded the mocking screen, no longer mocking.

It's like giving candy to a baby, it occurred to the universe-celebrated prose stylist.

It's like shelling eggs.

LORD BYRON

sends another innocent abroad, in terza rima

The President promoted his old mate
With a kiss upon the cheek for Condoleeza.
He sent her off to fashion Europe's fate
(In truth he would do anything to please her).
Then soon he called his secretary of state
For fear those Euro-bums would tease her:
'Now, Condy, you be brave and spunky
'With that two-bit French surrender-monkey.'

'Oh boy,' he thought, 'she's through with Helmut Schröder.
'I think our best hope lies with Berlusconi.
'We sure can't let a jerk like that railroad her.
'There's no one left to give her such a whirl as Tony.
'For all the wine and cheese with which he'll load her
'I know that Chirac thinks my girl's a phony.
'So bring home Condy now, it's like I'm missing her.
'And furthermore I don't like Henry Kissinger.'

LEWIS CARROLL

moves Alice into the 1960s

———————◄○►———————

'I know!' said Alice, who had made a point of always studying the daily newspaper. 'Let's form a popular music group!'

'Right on, little lady,' said the White Rabbit. 'But what are we going to call ourselves?'

'The Carpenters?' said the Walrus.

'You, Caterpillar, dear,' said Alice, 'you shall play the harmonium.'

'No, baby, me I'm strictly rhythm,' said the Caterpillar. 'But you want the Mad Hatter on drums. He makes Keith Moon look like the Dormouse.'

'I know,' said the Gryphon. 'Let's call ourselves the Turtles.'

'Or one could call us after oneself,' said the Queen.

'Hey,' said the Cheshire Cat, 'you want to try a line of Jabberwock?'

' " 'Twas brillig . . ." ' began Alice, who always remembered her lessons from the schoolroom.

'No, you don't *say* a line, you *sniff* it. Like this.'

'My word,' said Alice, 'this is the oddest powder that ever I saw. Something marked "Poison" is almost certain to disagree with you sooner or later.'

Alice took a great snort and felt her toves go slithy. Her

garden was full of flowering grass; there was whiffling in her tulge; they said that heaven was ten zillion light years away.

'Golly,' said Alice, 'what would my dear cat Dinah say? From here, the poor creature seems invisibly distant, almost unimaginably remote.'

'Yeah,' said the Caterpillar, 'like far out.'

RAYMOND CHANDLER

goes to Wodehouse country [1]

I had a short let at the time on an apartment in Berkeley Mansions. The rent was low because the owner was away in Pentonville and the rusty elevator screeched like a Palm Springs widow at a blackjack table. The super was called 'Fancy' Jeeves, the sort of stuck-up guy who reads Spinoza for the gags.

I asked him for directions to a luncheonette and wound up in some speakeasy called The Drones. I ordered a sidecar and a T-bone steak, done rare. Some lowlifes were pitching bagels at the electric chandelier with a spreadbet operation on how many throws it was going to take to knock off a crystal. I bought low from Oofy Prosser, a guy who looked like a blowfish in a tux, and shot clean through the flex with my Smith and Wesson.

Back in the apartment, I was counting my winnings when Fancy Jeeves came in and started plucking at my sleeve. 'There is a Miss Madeleine Bassett to see you, sir. The lady has been waiting a considerable time.'

---

[1] As schoolboys, Chandler and Wodehouse were near-contemporaries at Dulwich College, London.

He showed in a young blonde with eyes like the foglamps on an Oldsmobile.

'I don't do matrimonial,' I said.

'You naughty boy!' she trilled. 'I know you've always held a torch for me and now I've got good news for you. I have broken off my engagement to Augustus – which means I'm free once more.'

I sat down heavily behind the desk. Suddenly the day held about as much appeal for me as a stevedore's undershirt.

GEOFFREY CHAUCER

*celebrates the appointment of Geri Halliwell to be
UN ambassador on AIDS education to Africa*

Whilom in Dagenham there dwelt
A Girl of Spice that highte Geraldine.
Upon hir heed were locks of copper hue;
Gat-toothed was she, hir legs were like a
Longbow set to fire, and in her eye a gleme
That any sturdy wight might rue. In piercing
    tone
She shriek'd with other gentil damosels
In minstrel troupe; and yet full serious was she,
Well learned in high diplomacie, and to
Confound the folk who doubted her intent
Gan pullen up hir smok, and 'Lok,' cried
She, 'I have the Union flag upon mine queynte.'
Forthwith was she despatched from
Court as messenger from the United Natiouns.
Eek to the tribes of Indies and Afrik she
Voyaged mightily and took hir stande upon a
    stage –
Yet was hir stature smalle. 'By Christes bones,'
Quoth she, 'when that ye desirous be to swyve
    thy wif,

Tak care in caul or bladders greased to wrap thy
knob,
Such as men call letters of the Frankish
Kinde, for that ye gat not increase of poxe.'
A wondrous wench was she. Full fearsome was
Hir voice, yet of increase of it there was no
ende.

28

AGATHA CHRISTIE
from Murder in the Bathhouse *(1980)*

The door of the cubicle in the San Francisco bathhouse swung open to reveal a naked young man, lying dead on the floor.

'We're baffled,' said Sergeant O'Brien. 'But I have detained these eight other naked men at the scene of the crime.'

Poirot's egg-shaped head jerked forward curiously. 'So, Hastings,' he said, 'what mysterious link bring nine men together in such circumstance?'

'I suppose', said Hastings, 'the drought's caused a water shortage and all these chaps have got together to share a bath.'

'Look a little more carefully, my English friend. Do they have something in common?'

'By golly, Poirot, they've all got moustaches. I think they were all members of the same bomber squadron during the war. One of the poor fellows was so badly shot up by the Hun he can't perform his own ablutions and his old comrades have got together to give him a blanket bath.'

'A little warmer, Hastings. But our murderer is not a man. It is a virus.'

'A what, Poirot?'

'A virus. The HIV.'

29

'Not the high-speed locomotive, Poirot?'

'No. I will hexplain.'

Poirot proceeded to instruct Hastings in some of the ways of the modern world.

'Good golly, Poirot. Are you positive?'

'I hope not, Hastings.'

'But, but – how on earth do you know about such practices?'

'Hastings, you forget one thing about Hercule Poirot. Since all my life I am famous for my use of the little gay cells.'

SAMUEL TAYLOR COLERIDGE

on an ambitious building project

———————◄◦►———————

In Shepherd's Bush did Mister Khan
A new conservatory decree,
Where Alf, the master joiner, ran
The dodgiest business known to man,
For cash, no VAT.
So twice five yards of blighted ground
With scaffolding was fenced around
Where blossomed the odd apple-bearing tree
Beneath the gormless eyes of Sky TV.

But oh, that deep and structural chasm which slanted
Down the central ridge athwart the asphalt cover!
A nasty place! As holey and unwanted
As e'er beneath a leaking sky was haunted
By roofer waiting for his absent brover.
And from the floor, with septic turmoil seething,
As though old Alf in fast thick pants were breathing,
The ruptured water main was forced,
Amid whose violent interrupted burst
New-laid tiles vaulted like rebounding hail;
And sanitary ware rose through the glass
To rain down randomly upon the grass.
The shadow of the dome of pleasure
Floated finally in the hundredth week,

Where was heard the mingled measure
Of the subsidence and leak.
It was a miracle of rare device –
Two years in building, at three times the price.

ARTHUR CONAN DOYLE
finds new work for an old talent

————— ‹◊› —————

JOHN MOTSON Sherlock Holmes, what a fantastic goal!

HOLMES On the contrary, it was childishly simple. On perceiving that the studs in the Italian goalkeeper's boots were markedly more worn on one side than the other, I deduced that he was abnormally right-footed. Such morbid dexterity is common among the Genoese, whose mesomorphic body shape tends also to bow their legs.

MOTSON Very much so, in fact, Sherlock.

HOLMES I had previously noticed in a goalmouth skirmish the smell of pesto on the fellow's breath, and at the point of his utmost advance I uttered a traditional Ligurian oath. In the moment of astonishment that followed, I was able to slide the ball with ease between his conveniently open legs.

MOTSON Nutmeg, no less!

HOLMES No, basil and pecorino.

MOTSON As you say, Sherlock. So: a few beers tonight, then?

HOLMES I propose a moderate irrigation of the appropriate canal.

MOTSON Which canal is that then, Sherlock?

HOLMES Alimentary, my dear Motson.

CATHERINE COOKSON
moves into toff country

The day Maggie went to work as a maid at Lord Fitzgeordie's castle, the First World War broke out. The Germans invaded France and dug a long ditch from the English Channel to Switzerland. The French and the British dug one of their own a few yards away. Ten million men got shot, but then at last it was all over and the world moved into the Jazz Age.

Maggie loved working in Lord Fitzgeordie's castle and soon became his friend.

One day he confided in her. 'I am illegitimate,' he said.

'Whoah, soah am I,' declared Maggie. 'You know me sister, like, well she's really me ma.'

'Seems we have something in common,' exclaimed Lord Fitzgeordie. 'I was beaten at school, my mother is an alcoholic and my younger son was fathered by my late wife's lover.'

'That's like weird, man,' put in Maggie. 'I was beaten in the work'ouse and me dad never had a job.'

'Extraordinary,' returned the Duke. 'My pater never did a day's work either. Trouble is, the bounder's cut me out of his will.'

'Whoah, no, don't worry, man,' said Maggie, 'I'm the beneficiary of yer grandfather's mystery will. I'm a million-airess, like.'

'I love you, Maggie,' exclaimed Lord Fitzgeordie. 'Shall we get married.'

'Married?' exploded Maggie. 'I'm not even pregnant, man. Anyroad, I've not quite worked it out yet, but I think you might be me dad.'

NOËL COWARD

finds fun even in unlikely places

———————◄○►———————

I've been to a marvellous party
With Newcastle's lively front three.
We played drinking and snogging,
Spit r-roasting and dogging,
And other games quite new to me.
All the guests were invited to score.
First Kieron and Lee traded punches,
Then some girls swivelled nude round a pole,
While the manager sang in a chinchilla stole
To Jermaine, who wore stripes, being out on par-role,
I couldn't have liked it more.

I've been to a marvellous party,
With Davina and Kirsty and Cat,
Who invented a game
For the mentally lame,
Called Big Brother or something like that.
Some apes were br-rought on to compete
While we watched from behind a locked door.
A gibbon broke wind with hysterical power;
An overweight chimp ate a tropical flower;
An orang-utan touched himself in the shower.
I couldn't have liked it more.

I've been to a marvellous party
With Updike and Bellow and Roth.
We had to pretend
That we'd made a new fr-riend
In Salman, who came dressed as a Goth.
The shriek of the ego was bliss.
At midnight we heard from dear Gore
That de Lillo and Tyler were ter-ribly smashed,
But a naked Tom Wolfe was not one whit abashed
And at thr-ree in the morning, dear Salinger cr-rashed.
I couldn't have liked it more.

37

RICHMAL CROMPTON

*sees her ageless boy grown into an estate agent,
in the Summer of Love*

William's clients were waiting for him at the house: a terrifying stout lady of about sixty and her son, a drippy youth with shoulder-length curls and frilly flower shirt. William opened the door on to a small, damp cottage.

'Rather poky, isn't it?' said the stout lady.

'Hmm . . .' said William. 'It's got plannin' permission.'

'Permission for what?'

'Anythin'. Library. Swimmin' pool. Minstrels gallery. 'Smatter of fact,' William said, warming to his theme, 'it's haunted.'

'Haunted by whom?'

'The ghost of . . .' William racked his brains. 'Sir Hubert Lane. He was in the Crusades, you know. He came back here when he'd finished . . . crusadin'.'

'I see. So he was against Saladin.'

'Oh yes,' said William, 'Sir Hubert never done any saladin'.'

'Hey, man,' said the drippy youth. 'You ever thought about becoming a, like . . . hippy?'

'I'm not tunin' in,' said William indignantly. 'I'm not turnin' on and I'm certainly not droppin' out.'

When William got home that evening the door was opened by his live-in girlfriend, Violet Elizabeth. 'Thweetheart,' she said. 'I've got thooper newth. Every morning thith week I've been thick and thick until I've thcreamed.'

'Mmm,' said William. 'Must be somethin' you ate.'

'No, you fool. I'm ekthpecting.'

'Spectin' what?' said William.

'The thtork!'

'We'll have to get married, then,' said William. 'That means no more Friday nights down the Old Barn with Douglas and Ginger.'

'Oh darling, don't look on it as loothing the Outlawth,' said Violet, 'look on it ath gaining thome in-lawth.'

ROALD DAHL

Sees Uncle Oswald update Little Women

One day in April I was driving my Lagonda convertible through the New England countryside in search of the rarest orchid in the universe, the *Snotulosus flatulens*, the distilled essence of which would ensure eternal virility, when I ran out of petrol. Taking my crocodile skin suitcase, I knocked at the door of a modest house, where I was made welcome by a Mrs March and her three daughters, Meg, Jo and Amy. Over a bowl of clam chowder, I tried to decide which one to seduce that night. Noticing my interest, the comely Mrs March struck a bet with me after the girls had gone to bed. She would send one of them to my room in the pitch darkness of the night; and if in the morning I could tell her which one it had been, I should have my pick of the rest; if not, then I should settle a million dollars on the poor family. To a swordsman of my reputation there was no choice but to accept the wager.

In the middle of the night, I heard the door handle turn. I shall not go into detail of what followed except to say that not since the battle of Gettysburg the previous year had the earth moved so violently. At the critical moment, the girl in question was seized by a violent fit of coughing.

The next morning at breakfast all three girls wore looks of radiant satisfaction – as did their mother. Just as I was about to guess the identity of my lover, I heard a fit of coughing from upstairs. 'Oh,' said Mrs March, 'I forgot to mention my fourth daughter, Beth. She has a fatal illness. But pray do not alarm yourself. It is not infectious. Except . . . on the most intimate of connections.'

CHARLES DICKENS
has a shot at being concise

———————◄○►———————

Now for yesterday's weather in brief in the London area.

There was rain. Rain on the Thames where it seethed against the closed barrier at Greenwich, rain on the asphalt playground of the Winnie Mandela Infants' School in Haringey and rain on the umbrellas of the barristers' clerks as they ran from the coffee bars in Chancery Lane. There were showers on the Palace of Lies at Westminster and torrents on the Ministry of Procrastination in Whitehall; there were streams in the minarets of the mosque in Regent's Park and floods in the bilges of the pedalos on the Serpentine. Grey rain dampened the collar of José Mourinho's grey overcoat and drops ran down his neck; there were pools of water running from the meat pies of the lightermen at Shadwell. There was rain before lunch and storms after tea at Thomas Lord's cricket ground in St John's Wood such that the visiting convicts' team rued the day that ever it left Van Diemen's Land to visit. There was dampness in the feet of the secretaries running home in Tulse Hill, there was steam in the windows of the tailors in Penge. There were rainy tears pouring down the faces of the bare-legged young women in the alleyways behind King's Cross, and there was water slashed from side to side on the windscreens of their panders, as they watched from their dripping cars. From Hainault to

Epping, from Limehouse to Chiswick and from Downing Street to Coldharbour Lane, there was nothing but rain, rain, rain. In Whetstone, there were sunny periods.

Back to you, Alistair.

CHARLES DICKENS

sends Mr Micawber to Tin Pan Alley to meet

———————◄o►———————

THE ROLLING STONES

'I made the acquaintance of an inebriated habituée of licensed premises in the town of Memphis, in the New World, who attempted to escort me to the upper floors of the inn. I felt obliged to put up some species of resistance; until after the elapse of a short interval, when she had bestrewed my recumbent person with roses, then made as to evacuate the nasal membrane of the undersigned before going on to perform the same function for my intellect, leading me to the sad, though in the circumstances I think, Copperfield, you will agree, ineluctable conclusion that one invariably contracts dejection of the eponymous kidney from the female of the honky-tonk variety.'

'When I am being conveyed along the thoroughfare in a Hackney carriage and am assailed by the sound of a coster-monger making ever more vociferous assertions of questionable utility and I find it hard to conceive that he is a man of the same corporeal or spiritual endowments as you or I, my dear Copperfield, I find myself obliged to confess that I have yet to experience, to any measurable extent or degree, a feeling that will be only too well known to a young gentleman such as yourself – to wit, that of satisfaction.'

'It is somewhat curious, this internal sensation – since, Copperfield, I am not the kind of fellow who finds it easy to conceal the movement of his heartfelt emotions, while my pecuniary situation, as you know better than anyone, tends at the best of times to the parlous – though by Jove, if something were to turn up, I should certainly purchase a substantial mansion where you and I should both be domiciled. If I were gifted in the plastic arts – but on second thoughts, I should more likely find useful employment selling snake oil in Mr Sleary's itinerant circus! No, I know that what I have to offer is of small value, that it cannot be accounted more than a trifle, but it represents, alas, the best of which this unhappy man is capable. My endowment, such as it is, consists in compositions of a musical nature, and this one, my dear Copperfield . . . is for you.'

. . . and THE BEATLES

'A mere twenty-four hours ago, Copperfield, the travails that beset me seemed agreeably distant; now, alas, they have assumed the guise of a more permanent residence. Of the reasons for the lady's departure I remain ignorant, she herself having vouchsafed no explanation. I said something . . . inadvisable; and it would be the work of the merest supererogation to confess that now I long – in short, Copperfield – for yesterday.'

THE WASTE LAND

Said a Lloyd's clerk with mettlesome glands:
'To Margate – I'll lie on the sands.
The Renaissance and Dante,
Dardanelles and now – Shanti!
God, it's all come apart in my hands.'

ASH WEDNESDAY

The weight of the past makes me pine
For a language that's English, but mine.
No more hog's-head and Stilton,
And to prove I'm not Milton,
I'll compose with four beats to a line.

THE JOURNEY OF THE MAGI

We were freezing, ripped off and forlorn,
As we travelled towards a false dawn;
But the truth of the stable
Showed my world was a fable;
Now I wish that I'd never been born.

THE LOVE SONG OF J. ALFRED PRUFROCK

I once missed the moment to be
Someone not on the periphery;
But my second-hand life
Was too dull for a wife:
Now the stairlift awaits only me.

FOUR QUARTETS

For an Anglican, time is too vast;
A rose or a vision can't last:
It's a moment in history,
Our grace and our mystery,
And the future is lost in the past.

Ian Fleming

thinks even James Bond goes shopping

Bond lowered himself through a ventilation grille in the ceiling above the savoury dips aisle. He brushed the dust from the coat of his midnight-blue worsted suit and lit one of his custom-made Morland cigarettes with the three gold rings round the tip.

'What you think you're doin'?' said a bald Cockney, his paunch pushing at his ill-fitting nylon supermarket overalls. 'You can't smoke in 'ere, mate.'

Bond smashed his knee into the oafish man's groin, then, as he fell moaning beside the soap powders, drove the steel-reinforced toecap of his calfskin loafer into the red gaping mouth.

Ignoring the selection of instant mashed potato (Cadbury's Smersh, he thought ruefully), he walked through pet food and made for the wine selection, which was supervised by a young Mexican.

'Tell me,' said Bond, 'do you have a Chateau Gruaud La Rose 1990?'

'Eh, no, sir, but we 'ave the Sauvignon/Shiraz from Paraguay for £3.99.'

It was part of Bond's profession to kill people. He never liked doing it, but, he reflected as he fitted the silencer to his

.25 Beretta, regret was unprofessional. In any case, a cellar master without a decent Médoc did not really deserve to live.

He disposed of the body in the Healthy Lifestyle Options aisle, beneath a pile of jumbo grab-bag packs of ketchup-flavoured Hula Hoops, and made for the prettiest check-out girl he could see, a real honey in a pencil-line navy skirt and fresh white blouse with, he expertly assessed, a 38-24-36 figure. He eliminated the three people ahead of him in the queue by triggering a lethal dart from the adapted handle of his twin-exhaust wire trolley and found himself staring at a familiar face.

'Ah, Moneypenny,' he said. 'What are you doing here? Are you licensed to till?'

'Quiet, James.' She giggled. 'I'm under cover. Do you have a Sainsbury's Reward Card at all?'

'No,' said Bond, 'but I have a Goldman Sachs Plutonium card.'

'A packet of M and Ms?' queried Miss Moneypenny, looking up from Bond's basket and arching one eyebrow. 'Oh, James. Are they for me?'

'No,' said Bond, pocketing the sweets and dangling the keys to his grey 4½-litre Bentley convertible tantalisingly in front of her as he left. 'A little souvenir for the Boss.'

SIGMUND FREUD

works his magic in time for Christmas

———————◄○►———————

Fräulein Mary V came to me in the early summer of the year AD 3. A young woman of modest family, she was nevertheless a person of high principle whose character was described by those who knew her as 'immaculate'. She was suffering from amenorrhoea, and discomfort from a mildly distended abdomen; she complained of matutinal nausea and of cravings for strange foodstuffs, such as pickled herring with coal. Fräulein Mary, presented, in short, an almost textbook case of . . . hysteria.

Although she was at first resistant to hypnosis, I was able to establish that in a dream she had been visited by a man called Gabriel, an angel figure who told her she would give birth to the son of God. Since she was, and remained in real life, virgo intacta, this was clearly the suppression of a wish for sexual union with an idealised father figure. The herrings for which she longed were manifestly symbols of the watery and innocent past of humankind – a past to which she longed to return, where she would no longer feel confused or ashamed.

After several consultations which included hypnosis, bran baths and electrical treatment with the faradic brush, I discharged her quite recovered in August.

PS In a touching letter of thanks that I received at the end of December she reported that the abdominal swelling had completely disappeared, as had the nausea and the desire to eat herrings. She was meanwhile happily married to a Galilean tradesman and had indeed given birth to a healthy child. Clearly the hysteria had somewhat shortened the usual gestation period, since when she came to see me in May there had been no symptom of pregnancy. But such somatic anomalies, I have come to understand, are entirely characteristic of the protean disease of hysteria.

It was raining again when I reached his flat near the port. His landlady showed me through a hallway that smelled of gas and tapioca.

I knocked on the door of his room on the first floor; I found him sitting on the bed in his pants and vestments, darning his socks.

'Rex,' I said, 'I've brought you a present.'

'What is it?'

'It's a Life of Cardinal Newman.'

'I've read it,' he said. 'My mistress gave it to me.'

I looked round the little room with its single grimy curtain at the window and the unlit gas fire. There was a gin bottle on the desk and the remains of a pork pie and salad on the table. The room needed loving.

I sat next to him and put my arms about him; I could feel his heart beneath his chasuble. There was a sudden hammering at the door, which opened to reveal the sweating figure of Lopez, the chief of police.

'Had you forgotten, Father?' he said. 'The tramp steamer leaves at seven for the leper colony. I wait for you downstairs.'

'My dearest,' I said, as we heard Lopez clatter down the steps, 'do you love me?'

He looked at me with his fixed grey eye. 'Only God can love you,' he said.

'Go away then,' I cried. 'Go away and leave me alone for ever.'

His eyes lit up for the first time since I had met him at the seminary in Valparaiso.

'I hate you,' he said, as he turned to go. 'I think I hate you more even than I hate God.'

I heard the rain start up again outside on the cobbles of the dock.

THOMAS HARDY

writes a New Year letter after 'During Wind and Rain'

The kiddies did well for a start,
He, she, all of them – yea!
Teenager, toddler and boy
And one on the way;
Their faces beaming with joy . . .
Ah, no; the year O!
How the long days claw my heart.

In summer we bought a new car
An Austin Allegro – wow!
And had a great day at the sea
With not one row,
While we had shrimps for tea . . .
Ah, no; the year O!
See, the salt waves left their scar.

My book came out, just like that –
A three-decker novel – neat!
Brimming with comedy plot,
A quite remarkable feat.
It was printed without one blot . . .
Ah, no; the year O!
On my work the foul scribes spat.

We moved to a house painted red –
She, me, all of us – cool!
It has orchards and flowers
A twelve-metre pool
The brightest things that are ours . . .
Ah, no; the year, the year;
Now each one longs to be dead.

THOMAS HARDY

is sent to cover the big match

———————◄○►———————

A traveller across that windy heath would have seen Wimborne Minster start the game well with a brace of neatly taken goals by the poacher, Boldwood, back from a loan spell with Charminster. The return of the native did not last long, however, as when celebrating his second, he slipped on ground made treacherous by a leaking gutter from the roof of the main stand and broke his back.

On the stroke of half-time, Farfrae, the new boy from Ayr, was penalised for handball, though replays clearly showed that the ball had not touched him. Egdon scored from the spot and the Minsters' lead was halved at the break.

While the teams were off, heavy snow fell and the gale-force wind, which had been in Wimborne's face for the first forty-five minutes, turned round to confront them with its bitter fury once again.

Henchard, the left-back, did not return to the field of play after the interval, when he discovered that his wife had been delivered of stillborn twins. Durbeville, Wimborne's close-season signing from Auxerre, was ruled ineligible when the Channel packet was delayed and his registration papers were accidentally delivered to the wrong address. To make matters worse for the Blues, Fawley, the other substitute, was found hanged in the team coach.

Reduced to nine men, Wimborne Minster battled bravely against the elements till the sixtieth minute, when Winterbourne, a tireless labourer in the middle of the park, felt his Achilles tendon snap. Troy scored a tap-in equaliser for the visitors in the eightieth minute.

In the pitiless rain, Wimborne held out till deep into stoppage time, when Everdene, on for the fatally injured Boldwood, sliced the ball into the roof of her own net from thirty yards. The President of the FA had, in the Aeschylean manner, finished his sport with Wimborne Minster.

ERNEST HEMINGWAY
writes a Christmas round-robin

———————◄◊►———————

It was another year at 43 Havana Avenue.

The boy went to the university. We drove to the university in a car. When the weeks had passed the boy took exams. He took exams in media studies, sociology and theory of knowledge. He studied other girlish subjects. He passed the exams.

The girl was in a 'gap' year. She went to Pamplona. She lived among men and bulls. She has grown her first moustache. It is a good moustache.

The woman is expecting a child. The man was not expecting a child.

Now the woman is tired. Since last Christmas she has grown older, and heavy in the thigh.

She sits on the veranda at night and drinks beer.

'*Dos cervezas*,' she calls out. The beer is cold.

Grandpa is running guns from a small boat in Bexhill. He has a boy to work for him. The boy is lazy, but he knows the South Coast. He knows the beach at Winchelsea. He knows the safe landings at Hove.

Grandma stays home. She is not so agile since the thing with her leg. She lost it to a marlin off West Wittering in May.

Papa is working, still. He sits at the typewriter. What he writes is not good. He tears it up. Only when he writes in blood does he write real words. But there is not enough blood left in his veins.

So in the summer he did home improvement. He bought a seven-pound sledgehammer and a furlong and a half of copper piping. He built an en-suite guest shower room. The bidet is in avocado. The water runs from faucets marked 'hot' and 'cold'. The water is cold.

The shower cubicle said 'self-assembly', but that was a lie. It did not assemble itself. He took it back to the store, but you know how it is with the bums at B and Q. So he got a man in to do the work, a mulatto from Selsey Bill. But not for the tiling. No, not for that. The tiling took *cojones*.

Last Christmas we also wrote to you. The season was . . . Merry.

Thoughout the cold winter of 1934, Sibyl was at work on her fourth novel, *A Time of Loving*. The main character, Amelia Wishart, was a portrait of Ramsay MacDonald's mistress, Eileen. Tramways, the remote Cornish house where Amelia lives with her first husband Denzil, was based on Fisters, Ottoline Morrell's childhood home in Dorset. Denzil was taken by all Amelia's friends to be a depiction of Eddie Sackville-West, with whom she and Blossom Garnett had both recently terminated their long-standing affairs. Urged on by 'Sligger' Urquhart, Goronwy Rees claimed that he himself was in fact the model for Denzil, while Sackville-West appeared only as the footman, Spittal.

Sybille's beloved sister Victoria dominates the first part of the novel in the guise of Hester, the depressive painter, whose Mayfair flat – where in one unforgettable scene she entertains the lecherous novelist T. H. Wildbloode – was based on the Sloane Square apartment of Amelia's friend, the cross-dressing Slade figure painter, Camilla Gentleman. The curtains came from a design by William Morris and had been copied by Amelia from Dora Carrington's house in Wimborne Minster. Wildbloode was of course a portrait of the young H. G. Wells, with whom Hester had entered into an unwise liaison the previous autumn at a house party given by Vanessa Lytton-Duff, herself Denzil's mistress at the time.

Gerald's spaniel William was based on Augustus John's beagle, Maynard. Amelia's dress was copied from Rebecca's ballgown at Manderley and her Alice band was lifted from the Liddell family vault.

In *Sibyl: Lover, Muse and Artist* (Hogarth Press, 1978), Virginia Cornford argues that Bluey, the mute budgerigar so instrumental in Denzil's final comeuppance, was based on a canary belonging to Enid Blyton. However, Lady Ann Hastings told John Sparrow that the bird in question was dead before Sibyl could have met it.

There remains the, admittedly remote, possibility that the character of the budgerigar was in some way 'invented'.

HENRY JAMES

attempts a stand-up joke

――――――――◆◇◆――――――――

She crossed the threshold of the surgery, Millie Tarver, her Connecticut eyes lively with the breeding of a kind that, through all the long years and with whatever qualification had been disavowed by her countrymen, suggested to the doctor's eye with which the Prince was blessed, ill health, or something less than good health, or less like itself than more, far more, like the dimly perceived figure in a palazzo tapestry than it can at any rate at first have appeared.

'Doctor, doctor,' Millie threw out at last, 'I keep believing, or in any case assuming, that I am a dog.'

'I see,' returned the Prince d'Ambivalente. 'Or at least I shall endeavour to see, if you would place yourself upon my couch.'

The Prince was not wholly disconcerted by this tone of hers, nor was his perception so occluded as to prevent or in any case distract his knowledge that the hum of vain things, such as her lively clothes and fresh manner, might not so affect his *impression première* from which later insights might derive that, given the unavoidable allowances for the incessancy of effect of this exquisite creature upon the cultural saturation with which fourteen centuries of Florentine aristocracy had endowed him, it would come to be seen even by an epopt of blatancy to be based ineluctably and in the end upon a false, or at any rate erroneous, observation.

'I am to ask you', said Millie, 'if I might not persuade you to withdraw your instruction towards the couch which is, in my present circumstances and with whatever knots and anfractuosities I hope ultimately to unburden myself to you, dear Prince, contrary to my nature and my breeding.'

'And why so, Miss Tarver?' said Prince d'Ambivalente.

'Because', barked Millie, falling to her hands and knees, 'I am not allowed upon the furniture.'

DR JOHNSON

is still in the pub

'I fear our national game is fallen in such a slough as neither Mr Eriksson nor his 'prentice Mr Beckham may yet find strength or devilry to rescue it. Your health, sir. Only yesterday, peering through the inspissated gloom at the Middlesex town of Wembley, I perceived a small boy known to the rabble as Owen who ran prodigiously across the meadow in constantly disappointed hopes of contact with a compatriot, and his comical opposite, a giant the mob called Heskey, who each time he received the ball saw it rebound mightily from his shin into the safekeeping of the enemy; or else fell face-first to the turf, a Goliath brought low by the simple expedient of gravity. Thank you. Put it next to my ale, sir.

'Alongside him, the boy Haberdasher, nay, Dyer, paid 10,000 guineas for a sennight's toil, declares himself unable to strike the bladder with his other foot, and runs around the orb so better to position it upon the favoured right, revolving like a mule upon a Stafford treadmill. For such a handsome pension, sir, I had rather propel the balloon with my nose, scrofula notwithstanding, than to confess to such incompetence.

'Rearmost of this crew stood the woeful Mariner, nay, Seaman, whose unshorn locks bob upon his back like the tail

of Mr Boswell's pony. Why, sir, my friend Mrs Thrale was
never prettier coiffed than this fellow; though Hester, God
bless her, never wandered from her custodial duties in such a
reverie, allowing lobs to overfly her, nor flapped her pretty
hands at them like a sealion upon a ringmaster's bidding.
What? Yes, I shall take another quart of brandy if you please.'

JAMES JOYCE
makes a best man's speech

————————— ◄○► —————————

Enumerate the misdeeds of your oldest friend, the bride-groom.

Infantile and adolescent inattention to the Latin conjuga-tion of the holy fathers, necessitating manual application of the pandybat upon the rear conjunction and the saying of infinite-decimal rosy knees to Saint Pignatius of Disloyola and recitation ad nauseam of the Harvey Pariah.

What else?

A fondness for whiskey provenant in the distillery of Myrtle McInerney's, Number 43 Upper Leeson Street, taken solus, duplicitous and tremble.

Anatomise further the virile and hominal failings.

A weakness for fornication – several, serial and particular, with professional ladies, nocturnal walkers, painted Charlottes, scarlet Jessie-belles, principally resident, but only by the hour, in the rosiluciate section of Mabbott Street.

Nominate a selection of the obliging acquaintance.

Sarah Delaney, Sarah Molloy, Kitty Murphy, Gertie MacDowell, Andie MacDowell (a lack, alack, and solely in his solitary dreams), Eileen O'Leary and Sheilagh MacIlwaine.

Sheilagh MacIlwaine, the one-armed piston?

Indeed. In verity. In fact, Verity as well, now I come to think of—

Explain the manner of their conjugation.

Matutinal, meriodinal, nocturnal, bi-mensual, semi-annual and perennial; *in more ferarum*, in Morry's Ferrari, as horse and jockey, as coarse and mucky; coitus in situ, ab extra, in manus tuas, tuas, Domine.

Elucidate the reasons for the attendance of these several ladies at the nuptial mass.

I will, yes, my heart is going like mad and I said, Yes I will! Yes! Here they are, the very same:

Ladies and Gentile-men, the Bridesmaids!

———————◇———————

Hans T awoke one morning after a troubled dream to find his right hand had turned into a large mouse. 'Good boy, Hans,' said his mother when she came into his bedroom. 'Now you can book our holiday on the Internet.'

Two large men in raincoats sat Hans in front of a screen.

'Who sent you?' he asked.

'Never mind,' said the first man. 'Click your fingers.'

'Mmm,' said the second man. 'Microsoft Word has experienced an unexpected error.'

'What?' said Hans.

'Did your browser stop working?' said the first policeman. 'Or did you restart your computer without shutting it down first?'

'Or', said the second man, 'did you recently add a new item to your active desktop?'

'I don't know,' said Hans. 'But what shall I do now?'

'Do this,' said the first man brusquely. 'Right-click the desktop to show the desktop menu, point to active desktop, click customise my desktop.'

'Clear the checkbox for the item you added most recently,' said the second man, more gently. 'Right-click the desktop, point to the active desktop, then click show web content. Did you want to turn off your active desktop?'

'No,' said Hans. 'I want to buy a coach ticket for my mother.'

An hour later Hans had reached the site of Castle Tours. The screen froze, while a small egg timer whirled in fixed mockery.

Eight hours after this, his mother came into the room. 'Will you get off the line, Hans,' she said. 'I'm expecting a call from your Aunt Gudrun.'

'This thing doesn't seem to work,' said Hans.

'Get up,' yelled the first man, 'your message has permanent fatal errors. Come with us.'

'Where to?' said Hans.

'You will see,' said the second man softly. 'You have performed an illegal operation.'

RUDYARD KIPLING

offers advice to a would-be journalist

———◄○►———

If you can't write but don't let that deter you;
If you can't spell and know by now you never will;
If once you know the facts but still prefer to
Tell lies for fear the truth won't fit the bill;
If you can sub a piece about a women's college
And think it's fine to call it 'Girls on Top';
If the apogee of all your gather'd knowledge
Is the size of Beckham's shorts and Jordan's top;
If 'Whose — Is it Anyway' is your ambition
To shepherd into print day after day;
If you have once applied for a position –
And found they all would hire you straight away;
If you can mix with crowds and learn their mores
If you can meet with kings and break their trust,
If you can cheat your wife while off on foreign stories
But at 'love cheats' still feign profound disgust;
If you can never fail to write a headline
And cap it off with some moronic pun
Yours is the Earth when comes the final deadline
And – which is more – you'll be 'iconic', son.

PHILIP LARKIN

*prepares lines in celebration of the Queen Mother's
115th Birthday*

They mucked you up, your Mum- and Dad-in-law;
And then the lisping brother and his Yankee bitch:
For them the plane trees and the parties by the Seine;
For you the chores, the kiddies and the Blitz,
Snagging your slightly-outmoded shoes on the rubble
Of Mrs Snotweed's privy in what's left of Bethnal Green.

In the back seat of the hearse-like Daimler going home,
You scan the *Evening News* to see the outcome
Of your five-bob treble in the last at Haydock Park.
Another Railway Arms slides past, its table d'hôte a pie,
Stewed pears, pale ale and something final in the dark.

In castle corridors the draught disturbs dead forebears,
Balmoral princes in their lifeless gilt.
You cut the ribbon at the local 'media studies' centre;
A dozen sycophants grow flushed on Tesco's Riesling;
Your mincing courtiers make jokes about the kilt.

But Christmas time: your daughter mumming on
the idiot box,
'My husband and I . . .' – a phrase long lost to *you* . . .
Loneliness revives: the slice of lemon,
Three good goes of gin – and somewhere, beyond
the battlement,
A white moon glows; and you almost immortal, mortal too.

D. H. LAWRENCE

writes a brochure for 18-30 holidays

————————◄○►————————

LASSES: Don't be out of temper with the industrial society! Don't let your soul break and be bowed down!

To the Puritan, all things are impure. Do you long to escape from the land where the pits have scarred the valley? Do you crave the true warmth of working people in the landscape of an older England? Does the clank of mechanical civilisation fill your heart with the dread of soot and lung disease and small minds?

Be a good animal, true to your animal instincts. Wake up each day to find a woven coronet of daisies in your bush. Lie down beneath the stars and feel the world spin faster when you close your eyes.

Come with us to Mexico, Sea and Sardinia.

Fight always for the pure, for the holiness of passion against the dirt of the promiscuous sex relation. Must you always be matching your will to his rhythm when you can find the rainbow of eternal union and complete your own crisis with small whinnying cries?

LADS: Dost tha like ale and crumpet?

A. A. MILNE

gets gritty

Little boy kneels at the foot of the bed,
One nasal piercing in one little head.
Hush, hush, whisper who dare,
Christopher Robin hasn't a prayer.

Peep through my fingers, what do I see?
Hot naked ladies on Murdoch TV.
Wearing a dressing gown, reading a mag,
There's Mummy's partner having a fag.

God bless Daddy, wherever he is,
It's five years now since he gave me a kiss.
Oh Lord, don't forget to make me look cool,
Stealing Toyotas and bunking off school.

Bright golden curls on a bright little bonce,
Grandma's a pusher and uncle's a nonce.
Give me a PlayStation, Game Cube at least,
Big Macs and Pringles for my midnight feast.

Lord, let the Social send a man round,
Get me out of this tower block, down to the ground.
Hush, hush, whisper who dare,
Christopher Robin has gone into care.

JOHN MILTON

dictates a sonnet (in the Petrarchan style) on his declining powers at tennis

―――――――――◄o►―――――――――

When I consider how my forehand's spent,
Left in the veteran's doubles for a gentle hack;
And that one talent which I had and now I lack,
Lodged with me useless, in arthritic knee unbent:
To serve at speed my Dunlop with intent,
Now hits my partner's rear end with a smack.
'Does he expect clean aces from a frozen back?'
I fondly ask. But Partner, to prevent
My tantrum, soon replies, 'I do not need
Either your volley or your top-spin lob;
Your fluffed return with neither slice nor swerve.
For fetching drop shots I have all the speed;
With your knees you're confined to static job:
They also rate who only stand and serve.'

IRIS MURDOCH

*is told it's time her characters had real employment
in the real world*

Tamar began her new job, working at a factory that made scratch-cards.

She was shown round the works by the foreman, Lysander. 'This is Cato, our head of sales, north-east. This is our Tyneside rep, Amadeus.'

'Hello,' said a tall forlorn beautiful dull mesmerising young man.

'Production chief is Julian,' said Lysander.

'Which one is he?'

'She actually,' said Lysander. 'Over there.'

'All right,' said Tamar, 'and how does this scratch-card work?'

'The punters just try and try again, scratching and hoping, but the prize comes on a whim really, as a gift.'

'I see,' said Tamar, 'so it's like the grace of God.'

'In a way.'

'Coming to the Crown, Tamar?' called out Amadeus at lunchtime.

'No, thank you. I have brought my own.'

At her desk, Tamar made a picnic of cold baked beans with malt vinegar, grated Canadian cheddar on ginger nuts and some cold tagliatelle with dried oregano and Worcester sauce. With it she drank a sweet vermouth and apple juice, a combination of the nice and the good.

After work she went to see Gulliver, the head of human and Platonic resources, a man who had been married to her best friend Cassandra for fourteen years.

'Come in,' said bald beatific feline serene dandruffy Gulliver.

At once Tamar fell in love with him utterly and completely and without spiritual compromise.

'Come with me, Gulliver,' she said, 'to the seminary in Colonnsay where we can study Heidegger and Greek vases, get drunk on Rioja and swim naked in the Firth of Kant.'

'I am in love with you too for ever,' replied wretched twitching amorous angelic Gulliver, 'but for the next six months, my love, I'm on the early shift.'

[*Norah: Is this more like it? IM*]

GEORGE ORWELL

confronts the real 1984

It was a bright cold day in April and the miners were striking. Winston Smith glanced up at the telescreen where a woman in a blue suit with rigid blonde hair was wagging her finger at him as she recalled her recent victory in the southern seas of Oceania. He pointed the remote control at her, but the lady was not for turning off. 'Big Sister is Watching You' said a message on the screen. He sighed, as he pulled a sheaf of papers towards him.

Winston's job was to rewrite articles for *The Times* so that they included more references to prole feed and Sky Television. He was working on an article about the Balkans. After the word Sarajevo, he inserted, 'site of Torvill and Dean's recent sizzling, six-point, sextravaganza on ice'.

On the next page was a photograph of miners picketing at Orgreave Colliery, which he recaptioned 'Horses from the Police Three-Day Event team practise dressage manoeuvres encouraged by cheering Yorkshire proles'.

He felt a hand on his shoulder. 'Winston,' said a leaden voice, 'come to Room 101.'

'What's in Room 101?'

'Everyone knows what's in Room 101.'

Winston found himself sitting in a chair with blinkers on

his head compelled to watch a screen. On it there suddenly appeared a painted hermaphrodite wearing a black hat, pigtails, rouge, feathers and mascara. Winston screamed. And then the terrible noise began. 'Karma, karma, karma, cham—ee—lee—on, you come and go, you come and go . . .'

SAMUEL PEPYS

still loves London life

Betimes to White Hall where I did discuss with my Lord Falconer and Sir G Hoon the Queen's navy; though the colloquy was swift ended, there remaining but three vessels and they in dry dock for want of provisioning.

In the evening to the Cockpit where I did see a lewd play which pleased me mightily; was shown to my seat by a wench with electric lanthorn whom afterwards I impressed to dine with me at Mr Conran's coffee-house upon a leg of mutton, turkey pie, dish of fowl, three pullets and a dozen larks all in a bowl. On borrowing her miniature speaking device established that my femme was not yet returned from her Book Group and took the wench in a cab in Hyde Park where I contrived con mio manu toucher queyntly – puella absolument nihil negat!

Upon my return home found my wife in front of the electrical theatre in the parlour watching drama of four harlots in the New World. She cried, 'Samuel, here is a most apt title for your coded diary: Sex and the City'. Afterward, she, all complaisant, informed me she had prepared my favourite dinner – leg of mutton, turkey pie, dish of fowl, three pullets and a dozen larks all in a bowl – enjoined me to set to with a will. Meanwhile, femme, inflamed by watching

New World harlots, exceeding frolicsome. So at midnight found myself obliged once more to perform same acts that but two hours earlier avec grande passion in the Hackney carriage. And so at last – with troublesome colic and appalling wind – to bed.

HAROLD PINTER

once wrote an episode of a television sitcom

———◄○►———

Grace Brothers. The shop floor. The usual staff.
Enter two sinister customers, GOLDBLATT *and* MCCOURT.

CAPT. PEACOCK Good morning, gentlemen, may I—
GOLDBLATT Sit down.
MCCOURT They're coming for you.
CAPT. PEACOCK I beg your pardon. Who is coming?
GOLDBLATT The men. (*Pause.*) The men are coming.
MR HUMPHRIES Ooh, good-ee. Save one for me.
MCCOURT And who are you?
MR HUMPHRIES My name's Humphries.
MCCOURT No it's not. I remember you . . . (*Pause.*) You're
. . . Prendergast. Aren't you?
HUMPHRIES (*cross*) Well, no one's ever spoken to me like
this before in my life.
MRS SLOCOMBE These . . . men, whoever they are, I hope
they're not going to interfere with my pussy.
MCCOURT What's this about a cat? Do you see a cat? You.
What's your name?
MISS BRAHMS Miss Brahms.
MCCOURT Well . . . Miss . . . Brahms. Do you see a cat?
MISS BRAHMS No, not reelly. But I think . . . well . . . what
she means is . . . it's more of a metaphor reelly.

Pause.

MRS SLOCOMBE Oh no, not another pause. There's more paws round here than on my pussy.

GOLDBLATT Be quiet about your . . . pussy. No one's interested in your . . . domestic pet.

CAPT. PEACOCK Can I interest you gentlemen in a sports jacket?

MR HUMPHRIES You couldn't interest *me* whatever you wore, dear.

MCCOURT Yes. I want a Norfolk jacket. You ever been to Norfolk?

MISS BRAHMS Oh, it's ever so nice in Norfolk.

MCCOURT With wooden buttons. Side vents. Leather elbow patches. Like we used to have them . . . Before the men came.

GOLDBLATT When we were still free.

Pause.

MCCOURT No one's free any more.

Short pause.

MR HUMPHRIES I'm free!

SYLVIA PLATH

tells the story of Goldilocks

I am the doctor who takes
The temperature of each bowl.

Daddy Bear, your gruel,
Grey as the Feldgrau,
Pungent as a jackboot,
Rises under an ailing moon.
I have been sleeping
In your bed, Daddy.

Mother's oats are blebbed
With ruby stains of fruit preserve
Beside the glass fire
Of her blood-orange juice.

The baby's porridge bubbles
With a foetus eye.
I swallow the sins it is not
His to shrive. I devour
The cancerous pallor
With spoons of handled bone.

I plough the winding-sheets
Of each bear bed with my
Surgical breathing, as I die and rise
Three times before dawn.

My golden hair is electric
With the light of
Borrowed stars, spread out
On my pillow of skulls.

ALEXANDER POPE

turns his big guns on another soft target

I sing the goddess Bathos, who conspired
With Saatchi and Serota, much admired,
To cast Britannia in a sleep profound,
Into which torpor, with one mighty bound,
While gods of oil paint and Muses slept,
The Chapmans, Hirst and Tracey Emin leapt.
'No brush, just axe and chainsaw,' Damien cried;
'For me no canvas, just formaldehyde';
And so forthwith unseamed his hapless cow:
'Now look at me!' he shrieked. 'I've caused a row!'
And there above the tatty objets trouvés,
There played a turgid installation movie.
And lo! the work of Mistress Sarah Lucas
A mount . . . of cigarettes and is that . . . mucus?
Oh, daughter of Mnemosyne and Zeus,
Explain to us the meaning or the use?
'This photo of my boyfriend with the abs,
I think it's called *Fried egg and two kebabs*.'
Was ever sullen maid seen quite so pesky?
Turn in thy tomb, 'temisia Gentileschi.
Outside, Hyperion's light grew dark as pitch:
Off/on it went, on/off – with just a switch.

The Chapmans, Dinos and his brother Jake,
Were two more arty chancers on the make.
With plastic toys they showed the Nazi camps.
'It's new,' they claimed, 'and we're such naughty
    scamps!'
Must further cent'ries into darkness fade
Since Duchamps his upended privy first displayed?
If so, to us it would be no surprise;
For, born a goddess, Bathos never dies.

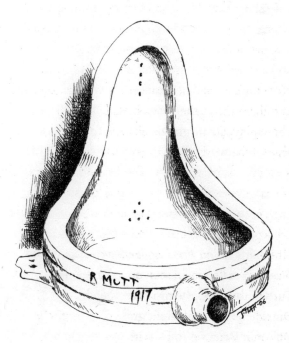

BEATRIX POTTER
confronts the facts of real animal life

———————◄○►———————

Mrs Fluffy Rabbit lived in a sandy hole beneath a hawthorn hedge. She had twenty-three sons, nineteen daughters and fourteen offspring by a previous partner. Her favourite three boys were called Randy, Ready and Peter.

One sunny afternoon she called them indoors for tea. 'Ready, put on your scarlet kerchief,' she said. 'Randy, your plus-fours are over there. And Peter, your yellow waistcoat – Peter, will you stop doing that. Mopsy is your cousin.'

'I'm sorry, Mother. She looked so lovely in her gingham pinafore.'

'Sit down and eat your lettuce pie.'

After tea, Peter put on a hunting jacket with shiny brass buttons and went for a stroll. Just near the foot and mouth disinfectant trough at the big farm he ran into little Flopsy, gathering buttercups. He allowed his eye to run up and down her gathered smock. She was his sister, it was true; but on the other hand, it was at least twenty minutes since he had last—

'Look out!' cried Flopsy, as a huge motorised vehicle thundered past. There was a squelch and a splat from further up the road. Peter hopped off to investigate.

'Oh dear,' said Flopsy when she caught up. 'What's that messy thing you have in your hand?'

'That', said Peter, 'is the tail of Mrs Tiggy-Winkle.'

WILLIAM SHAKESPEARE

writes a speech for Basil Fawlty

Good morrow, Major, what news of battles past,
Reunions, oft-told tales and regimental ties?
(*aside*) The man's a fool and deaf as Lethe's soundless
Waters sunk in sempiternal tacitude.
Ah, Ladies, must you be gone so soon upon
Your trysts and messages? Haply the charabanc
Awaits without. Sirrah, good morrow, the room
Is not to taste? The prospect circumscrib'd,
The lodging cabin'd, cribb'd, confin'd? Pray tell
Me, sir, exactly what your fancy had envisag'd.
A wood near Athens, the bright Illyrian shore,
Or Arden's forest dense, pack'd e'en unto
Its utmost bound with prancing unicorns?
Manuel, philosopher and sage of the Iberian
Coast, pray take in charge our noble friend,
Explain – as best thy tongue may serve –
The virtues of our hostelry, its charms—
But hark! What ghastly shrieking rends the morning
Air? 'Basil! Basil!' My poisoned posset, verucca
Of my heart, she-witch of wither'd dugs and venom
For her mother's milk. I come, I come, my bride!
May Aphrodite's chariot speed me to thy side.

DYLAN THOMAS

writes a cereal advertisement

The force that through the green gut drives the food
Is each morning taken mortal fibre, tock-ticking,
Clockworking, regular in motion
Of day and wind and
Under milk good soaking of rough husk
Of hill-high rough-age in tough
Tock-ticking, regular,
From the farm in the blossoming hill through the mill
From bole to bowel to hwyl
Where gesture and psalm ring—
It is your thirtieth day to heaven
Consecutive,
In all dark, all black,
All brown, all Bran.

J. R. R. TOLKIEN,
as so often, gives directions

———————◄o►———————

EPSOM ROTARY CLUB
Vernal Equinox Meeting
In the Ancient Halls of the Great Travelodge,
High Street, Epsom

Take A3 leaving Black Towers of B and Q to Westward under leaden skies. Take Morden Filter right avoiding accident and deathly spot at Hanger Lane, leaving Eastward in torrential floods of Kingston upon old Thames. Beware of road-rage, ram-raid and grey smoke of old mines at E-sher. Stop for mulled ale and folksong at dark waystation – but most assuredly at sign of Elf. Ford the mighty lowland ridge upon the Hog's Back. With howling gale from north by east along the southern circular, join M25, 4,000 leagues east and west, counter-clockwise, through the southern famine of the old wars of Gat-wick. Take exit south by north from second mini-roundabout.

Proceed with quaking heart to find main entrance to Travelodge (next to disabled parking) and enter in good cheer and fellowship.

Journey time: fourteen years, more in case of traffic.

JOHN UPDIKE

on how to boil an egg

<o>

Take one egg yielded by Rhode Island hen who stoically resisted the urgent courtship of the rooster; extrude its psoriatic carapace, held firm but tenderly above the pan, where the weakly bubbling tide appears exhausted by its repeated cycle from the headwaters of the Delaware, through the intricate plumbing of the human gut and the carpentered bowel of the Philadelphian sewer to issue once more from the kitchen's clacking faucet. Immerse the egg beneath the fretful surface, where you may watch its opaque shudder in the grudged wattage of the unfixed lamp. Admire the quotidian ebullience of its movement for as many minutes as may be yielded from your temporal overdraft, or until the mucous albumen has set – whichever you prefer. Marvel at the trembling of the aluminum handle of the pan from Norwalk's German hardware store on Pittsburgh Street, as the ebullience of American water makes it sing. (Remember to protect your hand in the miraculous cotton-jersey weave of the tea towel with its motif of New England churches that once quilted the Republic.)

Remove the egg in the cradle of a shining spoon, inclined at twelve degrees, and place it on a tray. Walk upstairs on planks of bevelled pine worn smooth by press of uxorious feet, and serve it to your neighbor's wife in bed.

EVELYN WAUGH
writes A Bluffer's Guide to Society

CHAPTER FIVE
The Inner Gentleman

Whatever the circumstances of your early life, even if you were brought up in North London, the Inner Gentleman can still be revived. Remember: It is never too late to buy the family silver.

1. Education. You were educated at Ampleforth and Trinity College, Cambridge. Brook no argument on this point; it is doubtful whether even the most resolute can overcome the disadvantage of having been to school at Lancing.
2. The family tomb. The Inner Gentleman will require a substantial mausoleum. While your actual parents may know nothing of the family before its arrival in Peckham in 1929, you may be sure that your forebears number among the great Recusant families of the land, and trace their lineage past the vulgar diversions of the Reformation and the Norman conquest back to the arrival of Saint Augustine.
3. Children. Children are an unutterable nuisance: greedy, ill-mannered and petulant. There is, however, no need to converse with them until they have reached the age of

majority, at twenty-one. Do not be tempted to baptise them with a modish Christian name such as 'Ken' or 'Tony', but prefer Peregrine, Septimus or Auberon. They will surely thank you for it in later life.

4. Women. There is no carnal imperative that the Inner Gentleman cannot subdue by a game of baccarat in the upstairs gaming room at White's accompanied by a decanter of Sandeman's port. You should not enter upon matrimony without the utmost circumspection, since the female mind will for ever remain a terra incognita. You may find it helpful to picture the unbridgeable differences between the sexes as similar to those between the clubs of St James's: Women are from Boodle's; Men are from Pratt's.

OSCAR WILDE

tries to be an agony uncle

From Mr T. Blair of Downing Street, London sw1

Dear Uncle Oscar

I have had a long off-on relationship with a man called Peter. It always ends traumatically when he misbehaves, but a few months later I find I have taken him back. He is in Brussels at the minute. How can I break my cycle of dependency?

My dear Tony

To forgive is human but to err is divine. For myself, I make a habit of never making promises that I can keep; it renders one predictable, and predictability is the godfather of tedium. By the way, Brussels is all very well, but not for the whole weekend.

From Anon, 17, of Birmingham

Dear Uncle Oscar

Every time I go out clubbing my face comes out in a terrible rash. Do you think it's because of the tasty Big Macs we have afterwards?

My dear Anon

A Mac is seldom big and never tasty. Your problem is caused by too much self-restraint. In matters of the mosh pit, a man should aim always to be like a pruned rose: half-cut. Try taking drugs. Remember: Ecstasy is life's revenge on death. Do not practise safe sex; rehearsal only dulls performance. But if you must, remember that a French letter tells you less about its recipient than its sender.

From John, 21, of Exeter

Dear Uncle Oscar

I am due to be married in two weeks, but I think I have fallen in love with my fiancée's mother. How shall I conceal it at the wedding?

My dear John

All men grow to like their mother-in-law; that is their tragedy. No woman does; that is yours. Incest is a triumph of hope over experience; and experience is the name we give to our lost loves. At the wedding, woo your mother-in-law by laying a trail of curried vol-au-vents to her bedroom door: it is the uneatable in pursuit of the unspeakable.

P. G. WODEHOUSE

goes to Chandlerland [2]

◄◇►

I pushed a moody forkful of waffle and maple syrup round the plate as I cast an eye over the sunny purlieus of Benedict Canyon. Ask those who know him best and they will tell you that Wooster B. is seldom a ball of fire at the breakfast table; and this morning I had a particular reason to proceed gingerly with the forking and shovelling. The night before had seen the birthday revels of one of my oldest pals, Scarface Cholmondeley-Plunkett, who ran what is known in the business as a 'numbers racket' in Pasadena. To say that the revels had been prolonged would be an understatement, a — what's the word I want? A li-something. Jeeves?

'Litotes, sir. A young lady is waiting to see you, sir. I took the liberty of showing her to the jacuzzi, where I believe she has disrobed, sir.'

'What? Completely, Jeeves?'

'I fear so, sir.'

To skip over the sprinklers on the lawn, skirt the bougainvillaea and let myself into the abluting quarters was with me the work of an instant.

Installed in the old tub was a young popsy with the lips of Nobby Hopwood and the general oomph and espièglerie

---

[2] See educational footnote on Raymond Chandler.

of Bobby Wickham. In short, the Wooster natural juices had not been so perky since the day I found young Pauline Stoker sitting up in bed in my heliotrope-striped pyjama jacket.

'I say, Jeeves,' I said. 'This is the life.'

'Gather ye rosebuds while ye may, sir.'

'Exactly. One of your own, Jeeves?'

'No, sir. It was the poet Herrick who so opined.'

'Well, he hit the bally nail on the head, didn't he?'

'There is a widely held view to that effect, sir.'

'Jeeves,' I said.

'Yes, sir.'

'You're beginning to annoy me.'

'Indeed, sir?'

'Indeed,' I said, and taking a snub-nosed automatic weapon from my dressing-gown pocket, I shot the supercilious fellow through the chest. Then stripping off the outer coverings, keeping on only the Old Etonian underpants that had caused my late gentleman's gentleman so much visible discomfort, I leapt – at last – headlong into those bubbling depths.

VIRGINIA WOOLF

goes to a hen-party

Hermione sighed as she descended from the omnibus and entered the gloom of the London public house where she had engaged to meet the two young women for what they referred to as a 'hen-night'. The swell of the capital rose up all round her in the sounds of costermonger, barrel organ and the brass band playing in the park. The eddying noise was attached to her, it sounded in her, it was a part of her.

The two young women stood at a wooden counter, a waist-high platform, a bar.

'What you drinking, Hermione?' said one of the young women. Her shrill tone, her small vulgar head gave her something of the sparrow, Hermione thought.

Hermione glanced down at her hand, empty beneath its white glove. 'Nothing,' she replied. 'But perhaps a glass of cordial. Elderflower, or mulberry perhaps.' The words made her long for the touch of the evening air in the walled kitchen garden at Buntingfold.

The two young women talked loudly of shags. Why, Hermione wondered? Duncan smoked shag; Lytton smoked shag; but why were these two common little tarts so interested in tobacco? Unless, she thought in a fleeting moment, they were discussing a species of cormorant.

Then they spoke of someone called Klein, whose first name was apparently Calvin. But she did not know Mr Klein. He sounded like a Jew, Hermione thought; perhaps he was a usurer from Cheapside.

Her head ached from the dreadful noise of the music and she laid her hand across her brow. She felt tired, she felt etiolated; she felt exhausted.

'Don't you like garidge, Hermione?' asked one of the little tarts.

'Garage?' she replied. 'I have no experience of it. I leave all that to Walton.'

'Who's Walton then?'

'My chauffeur,' Hermione replied.

This whirlpool of life, she thought. She was in it, yet not in it; she felt tired out by it all. One is beside it, she thought, one is over it, one is under it, one is . . . past it.

WILLIAM WORDSWORTH

does a Lucy poem for today's rapper

She dwelt among untrodden ways
Beside the skateboard track,
A bitch whom there were none to raise
And very few to smack.

Inside the car-park did I feel
The thrust of my desire;
And she I wanted turned my wheel
With looks and hands like fire.

My van moved on, mile after mile,
It roared and never stopped;
An ounce of skag and fourteen Es
Close by her hut I dropped.

What weird and wayward thoughts will slide
Into a gangsta's head.
'Oh, stone me,' to myself I cried,
'If my ho should be dead.'

W. B. YEATS
reports on the 2006 Ryder Cup at Kildare

———————◄○►———————

The restless multitude is pressed where
The wild falcon and the linnet wing
By Kildare's foam-thrashed sea:
More albatross than eagle, more
Eagle than birdie, less birdie than halved in par
In the afternoon four-balls
With Woods and Love.

Love and innocence is born in Seven Woods
At Sligo in the spring,
Though a five-wood's all that's needed with the wind
    behind.
I think now of Kiltartan's sons whose names
The English Belfry tolled in widening gyres,
The Irish soldiery gone beneath the mire:
Paul McGinley, Padraig Harrington, a tattered stick
Of Dublin rock upon the threatening fifth;
Christy O'Connor Senior, sixty years the pro at Lissadell,
Taken by the fairy as a child and shown the interlocking
    grip,
More overlapping than interlocking,
A public smiling man whose high slice
Loosed left-handed Eamonn Darcy on the world.

And in the final singles, as the sun falls behind
The lakeside tower, I watch him
Take the hickory stick. His limbs dance to a frenzied
    drum,
His unsure grip bespoke
By Lady Gregory's own assiduous putting stroke
Perfected on the borrowing lawns at Coole.

An old man is a paltry thing who hides his head
And cannot watch the white orb roll towards the cup.
So may it be that when I am long stymied
And gone beneath the divot
Under bare Ben Hogan's Head,
You may always pierce the veil and dream
Of Christy O'Connor Junior's soaring three-iron
To the gull-tormented eighteenth green.

∞ ACKNOWLEDGEMENTS ∞

I can hardly begin to express the apocalyptic gratitude I feel towards the people who have helped in the making of this book. I must begin with my partner, Fatima, for whose saintly character and transcendent beauty no words are enough. I am for ever indebted to Basil Waistcoat, an editor of genius, at whose hours of craft and dedication no sentient creature can ever cease to wonder. I must also thank my literary agent, friend and one-time (*sic*!) lover Sally Beresford-Knox; to her my gratitude is 87.5 per cent immeasurable.

May I finally thank Mrs Brenda Wigwam for the diligence and the dedication she brought to her unsurpassably brilliant proof-reding.